GAMING
TECHNOLOGY:
BLURRING REAL AND VIRTUAL WORLDS

By Anthony J. Rotolo

ReferencePoint
Press®

San Diego, CA

For more information, contact:
ReferencePoint Press, Inc.
PO Box 27779
San Diego, CA 92198
www.ReferencePointPress.com

LIBRARY OF CONGRESS CATALOGING-IN-PUBLICATION DATA

Names: Rotolo, Anthony J., author.
Title: Gaming Technology : Blurring Real and Virtual Worlds / Anthony J. Rotolo.
Description: San Diego, CA : ReferencePoint Press, Inc., [2019] | Series: The world of video games | Audience: Grade 9 to 12. | Includes bibliographical references and index. | Audience: Grade 9 to 12.
Identifiers: LCCN 2018046820 (print) | LCCN 2018051177 (ebook) | ISBN 9781682825563 (ebook) | ISBN 9781682825556 (hardback)
Subjects: LCSH: Games and technology--History--Juvenile literature. | Electronic games--History--Juvenile literature. | Computer games--History--Juvenile literature. | Fantasy games--Juvenile literature. | Virtual reality--Juvenile literature.
Classification: LCC GV1201.34 (ebook) | LCC GV1201.34 .R67 2019 (print) | DDC 794.8--dc23
LC record available at https://lccn.loc.gov/2018046820

CONTENTS

IMPORTANT EVENTS IN THE HISTORY OF
VIDEO GAMES

1978
Space Invaders, released by Taito, is the first game to introduce the concept of "lives" and a scoreboard to gameplay.

1995
Sony releases the PlayStation, which uses CDs instead of cartridges. The games also prominently feature 3D graphics.

1958
Physicist William Higinbotham creates the first video game, *Tennis for Two*.

1982
Atari has 80 percent of sales in the home video game console market.

1950	1960	1970	1980	1990

1962
MIT students develop *Spacewar!*, the first video game to be played on multiple computers.

1985
The Nintendo Entertainment System (NES) is released in the United States along with the game *Super Mario Bros.* This revitalizes the sales of home video game consoles.

1972
Nolan Bushnell, head of Atari, sees a demonstration of *Table Tennis* on the Magnavox Odyssey. In November, Atari releases an arcade tennis game called *Pong*. The game becomes an immediate hit.

1997
Ultima Online takes multiplayer video games online and sets the stage for future massively-multiplayer online role-playing games (MMORPGs) such as *EverQuest* and *World of Warcraft.*

2003
Second Life, a game with an expansive, player-created virtual world without winning or losing, is released.

2018
The market research company Newzoo predicts that the global video games market is almost $140 billion. It predicts that by 2021, the market will be over $180 billion.

2016
Niantic releases *Pokémon Go*, which becomes a sensation due in part to AR technology.

2000   **2005**   **2010**   **2015**   **2020**

2014
Microsoft purchases Mojang and the rights to *Minecraft* for $2.5 billion. Additionally, Facebook purchases Oculus and the rights to the Oculus Rift VR headset for $2 billion.

2001
Nintendo releases the Game Boy Advance, securing its place as the leader in handheld gaming technology. The Game Boy Advance sells 81 million units.

CREATING VIRTUAL WORLDS

Today was the day. The hottest new game of the season had just come out, and Sasha couldn't wait to play it. The minutes ticked by as the game downloaded to her video game console. Finally, it finished. As she launched the game, her television became a portal to an ultrarealistic digital simulation of the Wild West.

Her character moved with smooth animation, and the fabric of her clothes flapped naturally in the breeze. High-definition graphics captured every detail of the rocky plains before her. Each footstep left a visible mark in the dry dirt. On the horizon, a faraway town shimmered in the heat. Through her speakers Sasha could hear the whistle of a distant train echoing among the plateaus.

Even more stunning sights and sounds awaited her later in the game. The tiniest details, such as the rippling of a horse's muscles or the creak of an old wooden sidewalk, felt true to life. Connecting to her friends over the internet, Sasha formed a team to stop cattle rustlers and prevent a train heist. Voice chat let them feel as though they were really together in the virtual world.

Before she knew it, Sasha had been glued to the TV for hours. She had been totally immersed in the virtual world of the game. How do game creators make such thrilling and realistic

Video games can be immersive experiences. Players can feel as though they are standing on distant planets.

interactive stories? Behind the scenes, an army of designers, programmers, artists, and other professionals use cutting edge technology to make today's amazing games come to life.

GAMING TECH ADVANCES

Today's video games are complex experiences. Developers use computer software and 3D graphics create new worlds to explore. For example, *The Legend of Zelda: Breath of the Wild* is known for its open-world gameplay and stunning graphics. According to the game's

> **"The development experience was so great, and the game that came out of it was great. That's something I'm really proud of."** [1]
>
> —*Eiji Aonuma, producer of The Legend of Zelda: Breath of the Wild*

producer Eiji Aonuma, 300 developers worked on the game in order to revolutionize what a Zelda game looked like. He stated that the developers "took so much initiative, and were always looking at everything in the game with this eye to improve. . . . The development experience was so great, and the game that came out of it was great. That's something I'm really proud of."[1]

Inside these games, people meet characters that think with artificial intelligence (AI) and speak in the voices of human actors. In some video games, players can trade or buy objects either with in-game currency or with real money. Players interact with worlds using controllers that respond to precise movements. The atmosphere of a game is rich with sounds and music that help to immerse players in the experience. Some experts are curious about how technology has created more immersive games. Dr. Paul Cairns of York University researches immersion in video games. He states:

> *We're looking at personality, eye-tracking, people's sense of time when they're playing games. . . . One of the components we look for in immersion is emotional involvement. Becoming immersed is partly that you really care about the outcome, for whatever reason.*[2]

These immersive gaming experiences are possible because of advanced technologies including powerful computers, high-speed networks, motion sensors, virtual reality (VR) headsets, and more. According to gamer Chris Wiseman, "[Gaming is] a team-building and relationship-building experience where you can really learn about the other person."[3]

People all over the world have been curious about gaming technology for more than sixty years, ever since the first computers started showing up in science and military research labs. People imagined how these computers could be used for more than solving difficult math problems or processing large amounts of data. Some even wondered if computers could one day become a form of entertainment. As the technology slowly evolved, more advanced programs and electronic gadgets became possible.

These early video games set off a chain reaction of invention. What began as an obscure hobby has grown into a massive technology and entertainment industry. The market research company Newzoo "[forecasts] that 2.3 billion gamers across the globe will spend $137.9 billion on games in 2018."[4]

Today, gaming is a diverse culture. People from every country and every background are gamers. Newzoo expects that gamers around the world will spend "$180.1 billion by 2021" on video games.[5] For many of them, video games are an important part of life. Some people spend a great deal of time in the virtual worlds of video games. In this sense, gaming technology blurs the line between the real and virtual worlds. As the technology continues to develop, it will continue to affect the lives of gamers and the people around them. Virtual worlds will likely continue to feel increasingly real.

CHAPTER 1

WHAT IS THE
HISTORY OF GAMING
TECHNOLOGY?

The earliest computers were very large and expensive machines called mainframes. In the 1950s, most were used in science labs at universities, government offices, and military bases. NASA had a mainframe called the ERA 1103 UNIVAC. The purpose of mainframes was to calculate large amounts of information much faster than humans could. Mainframe computers were much slower than today's computers, but they were very powerful tools for scientists at the time. At universities, science professors and their students were fascinated by computers and imagined what they might be able to do in the future. Their curiosity soon led to experiments, often in their free time. It was popular for these early programmers to create games as a way to demonstrate to the public the abilities of computers. The first games, created in the early 1950s, were very simple versions of checkers and tic-tac-toe. Players competed against computer programs. Results were shows using lights on screens, but the screens did not have moving images. This limited the types of games that could be played.

Early computers were large and could only do basic calculations, even at institutions such as NASA (pictured). The ERA 1103 UNIVAC mainframe computer measured sixteen feet by fifty-six feet and took several minutes to process data.

In 1954, researchers William Brown and Ted Lewis created the first computer game that used a real-time moving display. It was a billiards game they designed at the University of Michigan. Soon, other computer labs began to design more complex games as well. These became popular attractions at open houses where the results of a lab's research were presented. One example called *Tennis for Two* was created by William Higinbotham at the Brookhaven National Laboratory in New York. That game used an oscilloscope, which is an instrument for displaying electric signals, to simulate a tennis match between two players. Players used buttons and dials to hit the ball and control the angle of each shot.

Computer technology advanced further, making new types of games possible. At the Massachusetts Institute of Technology (MIT) a new kind of computer called the Whirlwind was created. It was the first computer to use random access memory (RAM). This allowed for more complex programs. Soon, it became possible to create smaller computers that did not have to depend on a mainframe for processing. They became known as minicomputers, distinguishing them from the earlier mainframes. By the late 1950s, students at MIT had access to minicomputers. In 1962, experiments at MIT led to a major breakthrough for video games. A researcher named Steve Russell and his team created a computer game with starships battling in space. They called it *Spacewar!* The game used a special controller that allowed two players to steer their ships while firing torpedoes at each other. As the dueling spaceships circled, the computer simulated gravity to pull them toward a star at the center. The action was displayed on a new kind of monitor called a cathode ray tube (CRT) that was similar to the television sets of the 1950s and 1960s.

Spacewar! became so popular that it was shared with other schools across the United States. As more places purchased minicomputers with CRT screens, the game showed up in labs all over the world. By the 1970s, *Spacewar!* was the most famous computer game in the world. *Rolling Stone* magazine provided the grand prize for an event called the *Spacewar!* Olympics, which was the first video game tournament. The excitement over these early computer games inspired many similar projects in the 1960s and 1970s. A new programming language called BASIC had become the standard choice for creating programs on mainframes and minicomputers.

Table-top RPGs, such as Dungeons & Dragons, *inspired text-based video games. These RPGs had elements such as mazes, villains, and rewards to collect.*

Because BASIC was used in so many places, it made it possible for people to easily share games with others. One popular game was *Star Trek,* which was created by a high school student named Mike Mayfield. He based the game on the original *Star Trek* television show. The game was text-based, meaning players typed commands into the computer. It soon became one of the most popular video games available and can still be played today.

Text-based games became very popular. They were often inspired by table-top role-playing games (RPGs) such as *Dungeons & Dragons.* They were the first video games to include activities—such as exploring a maze, collecting an inventory of items, or solving puzzles— that would advance an adventure storyline. They pioneered the RPG video game genre. RPGs were advanced further in the 1970s by programmers at the University of Illinois using an advanced computer system called PLATO. The PLATO computers had high-quality plasma displays that were perfect for video games. The system was also networked, which made it possible for people to play games online with others who were also connected to that network.

Even with all the excitement over early video games, most people in the 1970s did not have access to computers and had never played a computer game. Some game creators wondered if games could be sold as a product. Two college students, Bill Pitts at Stanford University and Hugh Tuck at California Polytechnic State University, had designed a coin-operated version of *Spacewar!* called *Galaxy Game*, but the entire system cost a whopping $20,000. "The truth is Hugh and I were both engineers and we didn't pay attention to business issues at all," said Pitts, remembering the difficulty of creating the world's first coin-operated video game.[6]

ARCADE AGE

Until the 1970s, amusement games were made from mechanical parts and simple electronic circuits. The most common type was the pinball machine. A steel ball is launched onto the game board by a spring, and players press buttons that control flippers that hit the ball. Pinball machines and other mechanical games, such as shooting galleries and slot machines, were located in game rooms called arcades. Arcades eventually became popular places for kids to hang out, but they were first considered places for adults. Adults played the first coin-operated video games, such as *Computer Space* from the company Syzygy Engineering. The company, headed by Nolan Bushnell, later became Atari. Atari was one of the leading video game companies in the 1970s and 1980s.

Computer Space, similar to the earlier *Spacewar!*, was not a popular product. It didn't sell as well as Bushnell had hoped, and it seemed that the game was too complicated for the average player. According to Bushnell, he needed "to come up with a game people already knew how to play."[7] In 1972, Bushnell saw a demonstration of the Magnavox Odyssey. It was the first video game system that could be played on a television at home. It could only create three dots and a line on the TV screen at the same time. All of its games had to make use of those simple shapes. The game that impressed Bushnell was *Table Tennis*. He and his team at Atari decided to make an arcade version of the game. It was called *Pong*.

> **"[I had] to come up with a game people already knew how to play."** [7]
>
> —*Nolan Bushnell, founder of Atari*

Pong players controlled two lines on the screen to hit a ball back and forth, like a game of ping-pong. Computer hardware for the first *Pong* machine was assembled inside a wooden cabinet with a small black-and-white television that served as the game's screen. A coin-operated mechanism from a laundromat was added to accept quarters from players. The game's instructions were very simple: "Avoid missing ball for high score."[8]

This machine was installed a Sunnyvale, California, bar in November 1972. It broke down after only a few days. When Atari's engineer, Al Alcorn, went to repair the machine, he was surprised to find a line of customers outside waiting for the bar to open so they could play the game. When Alcorn inspected the game, he found that the old milk jug used to collect the quarters inside had filled up. Customers had shorted out the machine by trying to put more quarters in it. "It was sheer luck that the simplest game you could think of was what the market wanted," Alcorn remembers.[9] In its first year of release, Atari sold 8,000 *Pong* machines.

In the mid-1970s, a new type of arcade started appearing in shopping malls across the United States. These new arcades were designed for young people to hang out and play, often while their parents shopped in other stores. Atari was joined by other game companies such as Williams, Midway, and Bally Manufacturing. In 1976, Atari had another hit with a game called *Breakout.* Players bounced a virtual ball into a row of bricks at the top of the screen to score points. The game was designed by Steve Jobs and Steve Wozniak, who would go on to create Apple Computer.

A new wave of video games began in 1978 when the Japanese company Taito released *Space Invaders*. The game was a variation of *Breakout*, but its designer, Tomohiro Nishikado, imagined the action as a battle with space aliens. "I felt I could improve upon this by giving the targets a more interesting

> **"I felt I could improve upon this by giving the targets a more interesting shape and turning it into a shooting game."** [10]
>
> —*Tomohiro Nishikado, developer of* Space Invaders

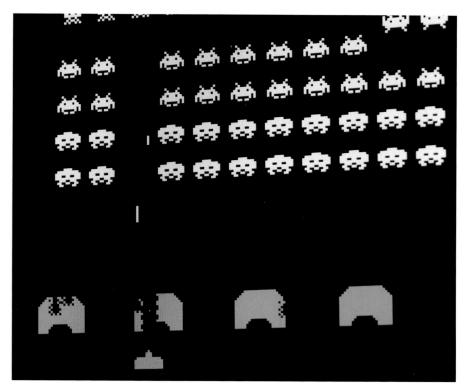

Space Invaders *introduced many new elements of gameplay. Players could shoot aliens and defend structures to get a high score on their local machine.*

shape and turning it into a shooting game," Nishikado said.[10] The ball became a type of cannon. Instead of firing at a row of bricks, a line of aliens descended from the top of the screen and even fired back at the player. The game had a simple soundtrack that players found very catchy, and it drew audiences to watch people play.

Space Invaders had several new features that made it different from most other games of the time. First, it had enemies that fought back against players. Second, Space Invaders introduced the concept of "lives," an idea that later become very common in video games. Players lost lives as they were defeated in the game, and extra lives

DONA BAILEY

Dona Bailey was working as a computer programmer at General Motors when a coworker introduced her to *Space Invaders* at an arcade. "He gave me a quarter and I lost all my lives before I could even figure out what I was supposed to do on the screen," remembers Bailey. Even so, she was intrigued by the experience. Bailey didn't know how to make video games, but she was a talented programmer. When she learned that Atari was making its games with the same computer processor she used at General Motors, Bailey applied for a job and was hired in 1980. At that time, she was the only female programmer in the game division at Atari. She became the software engineer for an unusual game called *Centipede*. Players had to blast a long, multi-segmented insect as it crawled down the screen. The game turned out to be an arcade hit. "I always thought it was really beautiful, like a shimmering jewel when you walked into the arcade," Bailey says. Today, *Centipede* is considered a classic of the arcade era.

Quoted in Barbara Ortutay, "Woman Behind 'Centipede' Recalls Game Icon's Birth," Yahoo! Finance, *June 30, 2012. www.finance.yahoo.com.*

could be earned by reaching higher scores. Finally, *Space Invaders* featured a high-score board that remained on display. The best players were identified by their initials on the scoreboard. *Space Invaders* transformed the video game world when it arrived in the United States. Midway, which marketed the game in America, sold more than 60,000 machines. Atari released a similar game, *Asteroids*, in 1979 to compete with *Space Invaders*. Soon, other types of games entered the market as well. Titles like *Pac-Man*, *Donkey Kong*, and *Q*bert* introduced new game mechanics such as navigating a maze and jumping on platforms or over obstacles. By 1982, arcades were packed full of game cabinets and players. The video game industry was worth more than $8 billion that year—double the sales of the music or film industries.

CONSOLE CRAZE

After the huge success of *Pong* as an arcade game, Bushnell knew that players would also enjoy the game at home. Atari released a home version of the game in 1975, which was sold at Sears department stores. Along with the Magnavox Odyssey, which had inspired *Pong*, and many other competitor versions, ball-and-paddle video games saturated the market. Atari alone sold about 150,000 home units in its first year. It was clear that people wanted more home video games.

Computer technology continued to improve in the late 1970s, with hardware getting both smaller and more powerful. Computer memory, embedded in individual game cartridges, made it possible to create game systems that could play many different games. Games could be swapped out easily, and multiple games could be sold for the same gaming system. These systems became known as game consoles after they entered the market. The most popular early consoles included the Atari 2600 and the Magnavox Odyssey. Although these early console games are basic by today's standards, they were visually impressive to players who had been used to games with black-and-white graphics or very limited color palates.

Atari secured its place in the console market in 1980 when it licensed a home version of *Space Invaders* for the Atari 2600. This was the first arcade game to be licensed for a home console. According to Manny Gerard, one of the Atari executives at the time, "The fact that you could take coin-op gameplay, convert it to consumer, and play it at home blew the 2600 to the moon."[11] Atari's popular game titles helped the company take over about 80 percent of the video game market by 1982. However, Atari soon found it difficult to sell more games. Consoles from many different companies had flooded the market, and games had become available on home computers as well. These early computers included the Apple II and the Commodore 64, which stored games on discs and used keyboards and joystick attachments as controls.

By 1983, the video game industry in the United States had crashed. Customers lost interest in the games available. Even Atari could not sell the games it had left in stock. The game *E.T. The Extra-Terrestrial* turned out to be a major flop for Atari. Atari ended up dumping hundreds of unsold *E.T.* game cartridges into a landfill in the New Mexico desert. Many people believed the home video game had been a fad.

In Japan, however, video games remained popular in arcades and at home. One of the most popular was the Nintendo Family Computer, known as the Famicom. This system also used cartridges for its games, but it was more powerful than Atari's machine. Nintendo used this advantage to create faster-loading games with new and interesting characters. Its controller was also different from the joysticks that were commonly used for arcade games and home games. Nintendo systems come with a controller featuring a directional pad, or d-pad. Players could navigate the game by pressing one of four directions: up, down, left, or right. They could enter commands like jumping or shooting using one of two action buttons.

In 1985, Nintendo released the Famicom in the United States, calling the US version the Nintendo Entertainment System (NES). The NES was a tremendous hit thanks to a game sold with the system called *Super Mario Bros.* Mario and his brother Luigi had appeared in Nintendo arcade games before, but *Super Mario Bros.* was new and different. Instead of having players try to gain a high score on a single game screen, the goal of *Super Mario Bros.* was to play through

Generation	Console	Manufacturer	Release Date
1	Magnavox Odyssey	Magnavox	1972
	Home Pong	Atari	1975
2	Atari 2600	Atari	1977
	Intellivision	Mattel Electronics	1980
3	Nintendo Entertainment System (NES)	Nintendo	1985
	Sega Master System	Sega	1985
4	Sega Genesis	Sega	1988
	Super NES (SNES)	Nintendo	1990
5	Sega Saturn	Sega	1994
	PlayStation	Sony	1994
	Nintendo 64	Nintendo	1996
6	Dreamcast	Sega	1999
	PlayStation 2	Sony	2000
	GameCube	Nintendo	2001
	Xbox	Microsoft	2001
7	Xbox 360	Microsoft	2005
	PlayStation 3	Sony	2006
	Wii	Nintendo	2006
8	Wii U	Nintendo	2012
	PlayStation 4	Sony	2013
	Xbox One	Microsoft	2013

t-home video game consoles are ordered into groups known as generations." Within a generation, video game consoles are roughly similar their computing power and sophistication. The table above lists some of th ost popular consoles in each generation.

Many experts believe that the Ninth Generation will debut around 2020. 2018, PlayStation CEO John Kodera hinted that a new PlayStation console ouldn't be released for another three years. Other companies have hinted a milar release dates at conferences around the world.

The NES was an extremely popular console in the United States. NES games such as Super Mario Bros. *and* Duck Hunt *have even been ported, or transferred, to more current consoles.*

a story. Mario's quest was to save Princess Toadstool from the evil Koopa. The game was the creation of Nintendo's legendary designer, Shigeru Miyamoto. There were secrets and surprises everywhere, which kept players coming back to discover more. "We had the feeling that we had barely touched the surface of this game after playing for hours," wrote one game reviewer in 1985.[12]

In *Super Mario Bros.*, players guided Mario through eight worlds, each more difficult than the last. They jumped, climbed, swam, collected coins, squashed enemies, and even threw fireballs in search of the princess. As the player progressed, the level would scroll from left to right, revealing the next set of obstacles to navigate. This type of game became known as a platformer. Nintendo and its competitors scrambled to make new and better platformers. Still, none could top the popularity of *Super Mario Bros.*, which is one of the best-selling video games of all time. According to a reviewer, "*Super Mario Brothers* belongs in that special hall of fame for truly addictive action games, the kind that keep you from being on time for supper."[13]

CONSOLE COMPETITION

In 1989, Nintendo faced its first significant competition when another Japanese company, Sega, introduced a new game system. The Sega Genesis was advertised as having faster game performance than the NES. The company called its technical advantage "blast processing." As its mascot, Sega adopted a blue hedgehog named Sonic who starred in his own series of platformers. Sonic was known for his ultra-fast speed as he raced through levels collecting gold rings. Sega used *Sonic the Hedgehog* and other action-packed games in marketing campaigns that advertised the Sega Genesis as a cooler alternative to the kid-friendly NES. "Genesis does what Nintendon't," the slogan went.[14]

> **"Genesis does what Nintendon't."** [14]
>
> —*slogan for the Sega Genesis*

The marketing worked, and Sega Genesis soon became a popular choice for teenage and adult gamers. Sega took advantage of its edgy reputation by offering some games with violent content that Nintendo wasn't willing to sell. This included the popular arcade game *Mortal Kombat*, which had become famous for its realistic blood and graphic violence. According to Gregory Fischback of Acclaim, which marketed *Mortal Kombat*, "At one point in time, games were just meant for children, and nobody really took them seriously. But it was with the launch of *Mortal Kombat* that people who controlled the media began to look at it differently."[15] Nintendo followed up the NES with the Super NES (SNES), which was released in Japan in 1990 and in the United States the next year. The new console featured a more powerful processor and improved graphics and sound, though it still used cartridges to store games.

In 1992, Sega released the Sega CD, an attachment for the Genesis that took advantage of new data storage technology. Compact discs (CDs) could store much more information than cartridges. This meant larger games with realistic graphics, better music and sound, and even live-action video footage. Several other gaming and electronics companies began experimenting with CD technology. "The race has begun to see who is going to set the architecture for the home entertainment system for the second half of the 1990's," said Bing Gordon, who worked for game developer Electronic Arts.[16]

In 1995, Sega released its next CD-based console, the Sega Saturn. However, the company rushed the Saturn into stores to get ahead of its competition. This meant the new console came out with very few games. As a result, the Saturn did not sell very well. Sony, an electronics company that was developing a CD-based console of its own, released the PlayStation that year. The PlayStation stunned the video game world with titles that featured impressive 3D graphics and digital video. It even cost $100 less than the Saturn.

With the PlayStation now in the lead, a new trend toward realistic 3D graphics took over the video game industry. In 3D games, characters and objects are assembled from shapes called polygons into 3D form. This meant that virtual environments could now be created. Instead of moving only left and right these 3D worlds allowed for deeper, more complex adventures.

Sony had already sold about 3 million PlayStations in North America by 1996. But even though Nintendo was late to the 3D graphics revolution, the company earned a powerful reputation in the era of 3D games with its 1996 console, the Nintendo 64. The Nintendo 64 was accompanied by a new adventure for Nintendo's most popular character, Mario. It was the first time Nintendo fans could play a Mario game in 3D, and *Super Mario 64* was a massive hit with longtime fans and new players alike. Game developer Tom Hall recalls, "It was the first game to really get 3D platforming exactly right. The gameplay was great, varied, joyful, explorative, clever, fun, smart."[17] According to one reviewer from the *Los Angeles Times*, the Nintendo 64 was "quite simply, the fastest, most graceful game machine on the market."[18] One reason the Nintendo 64 was so fast was that it still used game cartridges instead of newer CD technology. Although CD-ROMs allowed for more storage and often better video content, they took much longer to load their data.

> "[*Super Mario 64*] was the first game to really get 3D platforming exactly right."[17]
>
> –Tom Hall, game developer

HOW DOES GAMING TECHNOLOGY CREATE **INTERACTIVE EXPERIENCES?**

As video game consoles became more focused on 3D graphics and movie-style experiences, the growing popularity of personal computers (PCs) took gaming down a different path. Until the 1990s, most people didn't have a computer at home. They were still too expensive for the average person, and there weren't many practical uses for them outside of schools and offices. That all changed when home internet access became available in the early 1990s. A new world of information and connectivity was now possible with computers, including features such as web browsing, email, and file sharing.

By that point, computers had been used to play video games for many years. Many popular titles available on gaming consoles were also available on PCs. These PCs included special computer chips that provided enhanced graphics and sound. This allowed for high-quality gaming just like that of the Nintendo and Sony consoles. However, personal computers had one feature that game consoles could not match at that time—computers could connect to

PC gaming technology allows for many different types of multiplayer games. This experience can be different from playing games on consoles.

the internet. This opened the door to entirely new gaming experiences. The internet helped players to interact more than ever before, and it allowed players to modify games to their personal preferences.

MULTIPLAYER MANIA

Game developer Richard Garriott created a popular role-playing game called *Ultima* in the 1980s. As more people began to play games online using their home computers, Garriott wondered if *Ultima* could work as an online game, too. Until then, online multiplayer games were text-based. Players would type commands, and the story would advance as words on a screen. But when *Ultima Online* was released in 1997, Garriott brought the fantasy world to life with computer graphics.

Ultima Online let players control their characters inside of a massive online world called Britannia. For the first time, they could see all the action unfold just like in the single-player RPGs that had become popular on PCs and video game consoles. Players could talk directly to each other, plan strategies, trade items, and fight together. This created a sense of community that became a main feature of *Ultima* and soon many more games like it.

These games became known as massively multiplayer online role-playing games (MMORPGs). MMORPGs are known for their vast virtual environments in which players are free to roam wherever they like. Most of the characters inside the game are controlled by other people around the world. Everyone is connected over the internet to a central computer, called a server, that coordinates the online world.

At first, few experts believed *Ultima Online* would be a successful game. It was unusual and expensive. Unlike other games, *Ultima Online* required both a purchase of the software and a monthly subscription of $9.95 to play. However, players did not seem to care about the cost. In about one year, *Ultima Online* had more than 100,000 paid subscribers who played about 20 hours per week on average. The game was making more than $1 million every month for its publisher, Electronic Arts. According to Larry Probst, the CEO of Electronic Arts, in 1998, "*Ultima Online* has truly set the standard by which other online-only games will be judged, from both a technology and a sales standpoint. If *Ultima Online* was a separate, stand-alone company, it would be one of the few profitable Internet ventures today."[19]

That kind of success shocked the video game industry as a whole, but it didn't surprise *Ultima*'s creator. Garriott knew that the appeal of his game was in its online community. He said, "People are flocking to an environment where they can live an alternate existence, launching their own personal and business lives within a virtual world."[20] Some players chose to be warriors, battling monsters and growing strong. Others preferred to act as merchants, selling items or trading with people inside the

> **"People are flocking to an environment where they can live an alternate existence, launching their own personal and business lives within a virtual world."** [20]
>
> —*Richard Garriott, creator of Ultima Online*

game. Other players simply liked to explore the vast world of Britannia. This varied style of gameplay kept people entertained for many hours at a time in the growing number of MMORPGs.

The MMORPG genre was taken to the next level in 2004 when Blizzard Entertainment released *World of Warcraft*. This was the fourth chapter of the company's popular strategy game series, *Warcraft*, but it was the first to use online gaming in an open world. The video game community did not expect much from this new release. "When Blizzard first announced that it was working on a massively multiplayer online game," wrote one reviewer, "the first thought that ran through my mind was 'Why? Blizzard has no experience in this area.'"[21]

But to the surprise of many, *World of Warcraft*, sometimes called *WoW* for short, turned out to be a big success. It wasn't because of advanced graphics or complicated gameplay. *World of Warcraft* was a hit because, unlike other MMORPGs, it was an action-packed adventure that was easy for anyone to play. Blizzard had observed other MMORPGs and learned what frustrated players. In *World of Warcraft*, players who died in battle didn't lose their hard work, and they could get right back to playing again within minutes. Even though the graphics were less advanced than some other games, they were still beautiful. And these simpler graphics meant the game had short load times and did not crash very often. "I can honestly say that *WoW* is friendly to everybody," raved one game reviewer. "Everything from the colorful art style to the endearing player animations, to the countless quirks of personality makes *WoW* an inviting experience."[22]

World of Warcraft soon became the most successful MMORPG of all time. Since 2004, there have been several expansions to the game, each adding new stories and features. In 2008, Blizzard announced there were more than 10 million active players of *WoW*. In 2014, ten years after its release, *World of Warcraft* was still popular, and more than 100 million people had played the game.

THE FPS GENRE GOES ONLINE

The popularity of online gameplay pushed other types of video games in that direction. This included first-person shooter (FPS) games, such as *Doom*, which were a favorite type of game on both computers and consoles. FPS games are viewed through the eyes of the main character, and usually only the character's hands or weapon are visible as they navigate through an open environment filled with enemies. According to a 2018 survey by the Entertainment Software Association, shooter games are the most-played type of multiplayer game. By going online, FPS games took on an entirely new dimension. Instead of shooting at computer-controlled creatures, players could now battle against each other.

Quake was a groundbreaking FPS game released by id Software in 1996. It was a follow-up to the Doom series that helped make FPS games popular. *Doom* and similar games were enjoyed mostly as single-player experiences. But the Quake series took advantage of home networking and internet connections. Multiplayer battles became far more appealing than single-player mode. Another selling point of *Quake* was its software, which was a major advancement in 3D graphics. Previous first-person games had only simulated 3D mazes using flat, 2D graphics. The 3D world of *Quake* had more depth and realism.

VIRTUAL EXPERIENCES AND REAL-LIFE BEHAVIOR

What is it about virtual worlds that attract so many people? Some experts believe that game worlds help fulfill important human needs. Playing games can offer feelings of excitement and deep engagement. Games can make people feel heroic, powerful, and more connected to others. Gamers often must learn to cooperate, collaborate, and provide leadership or help to others in order to be successful in multiplayer challenges. These virtual experiences can help people practice for using the same skills in real-life situations.

But advancements in technology are making virtual experiences feel more and more realistic. For some people, these realistic virtual worlds have become addictive. In 2018, the World Health Organization added Gaming Disorder to its list of official diseases. Those who suffer from Gaming Disorder lose control over their gaming habits, and they keep playing even if it keeps them from doing other important things such as eating, sleeping, spending time with family and friends, or going to work or school.

Quake's online community grew into an active place for fans of FPS games. Players could arrange matches using a built-in chat feature. The action was fast-paced and exciting, and the 3D levels made it possible for players to run, jump, hide, and surprise their friends during a battle. The game's sound effects and music helped create a uniquely spooky atmosphere that added to the excitement.

Even though *Quake*'s online action was a big selling point, there was much more to the game's popularity online. Fans of *Quake* were given access to the game's underlying computer code so that players could create new levels and features all on their own. A community of amateur game developers began sharing their creations over the internet. Other players could download these updates to their own computers and make creative additions to the game. These changes, called modifications or mods, changed the video game world forever.

MOD LIFE

When gamers change the code, they can personalize the game. Modding separates PC gaming from the console market. Even though online multiplayer features are available on more recent consoles, many gamers prefer to play on their computers in order to create their own mods and access mods created by others.

As early as the 1980s, people were experimenting with modding. The popularity of these mods prompted id Software to release *Doom* with a file that gave players easy access to make their own levels. This was so popular that in 1994, id Software decided to make simple tools so that even more people could modify the game. Soon, amateur coders were adding new monsters and features to *Doom*.

When id Software's developers began working on *Quake*, they knew it would be important to include mod features in the game.

To accomplish this, developer John Carmack created a programming language called QuakeC that was built right into the game itself. This allowed modders to directly access the game's software so they could dramatically change the entire game. This type of mod that turns one game into a completely different game is called a total conversion. One total conversion mod for *Quake,* called *AirQuake*, transformed the FPS game into an aerial battle between flying ships.

Some mods even become so popular that game development companies acquire them and release them as new games. For example, one of the most popular *Quake* mods converted the game into a giant game of capture-the-flag. Teams tried to steal each other's flags. This mod was eventually acquired by Valve Software and released as its own game, *Team Fortress*.

In 1998, Valve's FPS *Half-Life* became the inspiration for one of the most successful game mods of all time. Amateur programmer Minh Le and modder Jess Cliffe transformed the alien-blasting *Half-Life* into a game about counterterrorism called *Counter-Strike*. "It was great because that was when I got really interested in making games and I knew that I wanted to do this for a living," Le said.[23] *Counter-Strike* became a major hit

> **"[Modding] was great because that was when I got really interested in making games and I knew that I wanted to do this for a living." [23]**
>
> —*Minh Le, programmer and co-creator of* Counter-Strike

The sequel to Counter-Strike, Counter-Strike: Global Offensive, *is a popular E-Sports game. It is played at E-Sports tournaments around the world.*

with other players online, and that caught the attention of Valve CEO Gabe Newell, who hired Le and Cliffe. Valve acquired the rights to *Counter-Strike*, and the game has become a hugely successful franchise. As of 2016, more than 650,000 players were still active on the game's sequel, *Counter-Strike: Global Offensive*.

Newell believes that modding games is one of the best ways for aspiring video game developers to find jobs in the industry. He said, "The fact that somebody has been able to build something . . . and then deal with the gush of responses you get, filter through that in a useful and productive way . . . is really the core of product design and development in our world."[24] Le and Cliffe's story of success is just one example of many mod developers who have been hired by top video game companies.

SECOND LIFE AND A VIRTUAL WORLD

In 2003, the online game *Second Life* made mods an important part of its virtual world. Developed by Linden Labs in San Francisco, California, *Second Life* has many of the same features as MMORPGs, including a vast 3D environment, thousands of locations, and players represented by their avatars. However, in *Second Life* there are no set storylines or goals. Players simply interact with one another. "We don't see this as a game," *Second Life* founder Philip Rosedale said. "We see it as a platform that is, in many ways, better than the real world."[25]

In *Second Life*, nearly everything within the virtual world is created by the players. This includes buildings and theme parks along with avatar clothing and millions of personal items. Nearly anything can be designed using the game's built-in programming language, Linden Scripting Language. These things can be traded or sold within the game using real money. *Second Life* has its own currency known as Linden Dollars, which can be exchanged for real-world currencies. "The amazing thing is that if you give people the ability to make things, obviously they're going to value those things," Rosedale said in 2006.[26] By 2007, Linden Labs reported that *Second Life* had over 1 million residents.

If *Second Life* is not a game in which people can win, then why do people use it? *Second Life* is an active marketplace. Rosedale added that the ability for users to design and sculpt the world plays a large part in people's desire to play, stating, "All that's needed is cleverness. All that's necessary is intelligence, skill, design."[27] Some residents have earned considerable cash buying and selling inside *Second Life*. Ailin Graef, whose *Second Life* avatar is named Anshe Chung, began her business by coding different elements in *Second Life*. She used her profits to buy up pieces of virtual land and then developed the property with beautiful landscapes and buildings so that it could be sold for much higher prices. By 2005, Graef was making an estimated $150,000 per year. She became the world's first millionaire with an entirely virtual business. Her success earned worldwide attention, and her avatar appeared on the cover of *BusinessWeek* magazine. Graef proved that virtual worlds could be used for much more than playing games. "What I found [in *Second Life*] were real people with real emotions and real friendships," Graef said. "I also found the economy was very real."[28] Shortly after Graef's financial success was publicized, Linden Labs received millions of dollars from investors, including Amazon CEO Jeff Bezos. As Hunter Walk, one of *Second Life*'s original developers put it, "In your first life you don't necessarily get to fly. Here you can fly."[29] However, *Second Life* did not continue to grow. The number of Second Life users peaked at around one million in 2007. As of December 2017, there were only 800,000 monthly *Second Life* users.

> **"In your first life you don't necessarily get to fly. Here you can fly."** [29]
>
> —*Hunter Walk, one of the original developers of Second Life*

MASTER OF MINES

"The act of borrowing ideas is integral to the creative process," says programmer Zachary Barth. "That's how it works."[30] Barth would certainly know. In 2009, he created a game called *Infiniminer* that involved mining and building in a virtual world made of blocks. Barth's *Infiniminer* gained a small but dedicated following with gamers around the world. Unfortunately, his plans to continue developing the game were dashed when his source code was leaked on the internet shortly after he released the game. In response, Barth gave *Infiniminer*'s fans permission to use the code however they liked. One of those fans was Swedish programmer Markus "Notch" Persson. His version of the mining game would soon make video game history.

In high school, Persson created his own version of *Pong*. Soon, he would create many more games of his own, eventually landing a job with game development company Midasplayer, now called King.com, which is best known for making *Candy Crush*. Even though Persson had achieved his goal of becoming a game designer, he was unhappy at work. He dreamed of making games independently so that he could be in control of the entire product. When Persson saw *Infiniminer* for the first time, he knew he'd found the right template for his ideas. He was fascinated by *Infiniminer*'s virtual world, in which every block could be mined and used to build something else. He also liked how the game's graphics were very basic shapes instead of the more common style of smooth, 3D graphics. Persson immediately started working on his own version of *Infiniminer*, changing the game so that it was played from a first-person view. He also made the graphics blockier. In May 2009, he posted an early look at his game on YouTube and said, "This is a very early test of an *Infiniminer* clone I'm working on."[31]

Persson decided to call his game *Minecraft*. After posting the first version online, Persson was overwhelmed by the response. By adding more types of blocks, characters, and a multiplayer mode, he was able to grow the audience for *Minecraft*. Within one year of its release, more than 20,000 players had paid for access to *Minecraft*. Persson started his own company, Mojang Specifications.

Minecraft and its distinctive style became a pop culture icon. It captured the attention of an enthusiastic mod community, and soon new features and styles of gameplay sprung up. Many of these mods were adopted into the official game. By 2011, *Minecraft* had more than a million users. Soon the game was made available on consoles as well, arriving first on the Xbox 360 and later on the PlayStation 3. There was even merchandise, including a *Minecraft* Lego set.

All of this success was beyond anything Persson could have ever imagined for his video game. *"Minecraft* certainly became a huge hit, and people are telling me it's changing games," Persson said. "I never meant for it to do either."[32] Unfortunately for Persson, *Minecraft*'s widespread success meant his goal of developing games independently was slipping away. He stated, "I'm not a CEO. I'm a nerdy computer programmer who likes to have opinions on Twitter."[33] In June 2014, Persson tweeted, "Anyone want to buy my share of Mojang."[34] That tweet received many offers from video game companies, but Microsoft won the bidding war for *Minecraft*. In November 2014, Microsoft bought Mojang for $2.5 billion. *Minecraft* quickly expanded across more gaming platforms, including

> **"Minecraft certainly became a huge hit, and people are telling me it's changing games. I never meant for it to do either."** [32]
>
> —Markus "Notch" Persson, creator *of* Minecraft

Minecraft *is available for mobile devices in addition to consoles. Players can do many of the same activities in both versions of the game, such as building houses and taming wild creatures.*

smartphones and VR headsets. As of 2018, *Minecraft* had more than 140 million paid accounts and was one of the most popular video games of all time. There was even a *Minecraft* movie in the works.

With a large and active mod community, millions of fans watching *Minecraft* gaming videos on Twitch and YouTube, and even an educational version of the game, *Minecraft* has become a platform for creativity, innovation, and learning. Persson says that whatever comes next will be built by *Minecraft*'s players. "In one sense, it belongs to Microsoft now," he says. "In a much bigger sense, it's belonged to all of you for a long time, and that will never change."[35]

CHAPTER
3

HOW HAS GAMING TECHNOLOGY BECOME MOBILE?

Mobile gaming technology has been a popular trend since the end of the twentieth century. Today, smartphones and tablets allow many people to easily play video games. But mobile gaming technology first became popular in 1989, when the Nintendo Game Boy instantly became a top-selling item. It remained the hottest handheld gaming device for more than two decades. With its 2.6-inch (6.6 cm) green-and-black screen, the Game Boy was extremely simplistic in comparison to today's mobile technology. But the Game Boy's mobility, rather than cutting-edge hardware or software, is what attracted many users.

With the Game Boy, players could take their favorite games with them anywhere. This simple change transformed gaming into a casual activity. Players were no longer attached to their television sets or home computers. Instead of needing a cumbersome power cord, a Game Boy just required a few batteries. For the first time, a few spare minutes waiting in line or a long car ride could become an opportunity to play a game. Millions of people in America and around the world became hooked on games such as *Tetris*. This puzzle game

The Nintendo Switch is a handheld console with many games. Some games, such as Mario Kart 8, are part of long-running Nintendo franchises.

was packaged with the original Game Boy and quickly became the best-selling video game of all time.

The Game Boy and the updated Game Boy Color sold more than 118 million units worldwide. There were hundreds of games to choose from, including Nintendo classics such as *Mario Kart, Super Mario Land*, and several new Legend of Zelda adventures. Then, in 1996, Nintendo unveiled Pokémon, a new game series that would take the handheld gaming world by storm.

Pokémon is a series of RPGs created by Japanese developer Satoshi Tajiri. Players must capture and collect magical creatures—called Pokémon, short for pocket monsters—and train them for battle. The best way to be a successful Pokémon collector and trainer was to trade the creatures with friends. By hooking up a cable between

> **"I imagined an insect moving back and forth across the cable. My idea was for information to go back and forth, to be shared."** [36]
>
> —Satoshi Tajiri, creator of Pokémon

Game Boys, players could swap Pokémon and even battle against each other. "I imagined an insect moving back and forth across the cable," Tajiri said. "My idea was for information to go back and forth, to be shared."[36] This process made Pokémon games a social experience. To make the collecting more exciting and to sell more games, Nintendo developer Shigeru Miyamoto suggested creating multiple Pokémon titles that included different sets of monsters to capture in each. This led to the color-themed series of games that included *Pokémon Red*, *Pokémon Blue*, and *Pokémon Yellow*. Soon, Pokémon became an international sensation. Today, it is the second-best-selling game series in history behind Nintendo's Super Mario franchise.

Competitor devices such as the Sega Game Gear and Atari Lynx offered more advanced hardware or graphics, but they couldn't match the popularity of the Game Boy. Nintendo maintained its lead with the 2001 release of the Game Boy Advance, which featured a better screen along with improved graphics and sound. The new handheld sold an impressive 81 million units. Some experts believed that cell phones would eventually become a worthy challenger to Nintendo, but the phones of the early 2000s made for awkward gaming devices. In 2003, phone-maker Nokia even tried offering a cell phone called the

N-Gage that was designed to work like a portable game system, but reviewers disliked it and it didn't sell well. At the turn of the millennium, Nintendo remained the undisputed leader of handheld games.

ATTACK OF THE PHONES

As a college student at Syracuse University in the 1990s, Dennis Crowley wondered what it would be like if he could interact with objects and places in his environment in the same way that game characters like Mario would do. He thought, could a real person earn points or complete challenges by visiting certain places? If so, perhaps that could be a whole new way to play games with friends.

A few years later, around the year 2000, Crowley's idea became a part of his work as a graduate student at New York University. For his thesis project in the Interactive Telecommunications program, Crowley teamed up with his friend, Alex Rainert, with the goal of turning the real world into a kind of mobile game. Using the basic cell phones of that time, they designed a technology that allowed users to text their locations to an online service which would notify them of friends and interesting places nearby. They called it Dodgeball.

In the days before apps and touchscreen phones, Dodgeball was a breakthrough mobile tool. Crowley had shown that mobile phones could be used for much more than just placing a call. Google thought so, too. When the internet technology company noticed Dodgeball in 2005, it bought Crowley's company and hired him to work for them. Unfortunately, Crowley's vision was still ahead of its time, and mobile technology would not catch up for several years. After a frustrating period at Google, Dodgeball was eventually shut down in 2009. Crowley soon left Google in search of a new way to bring his real-world location game to life.

The answer to Crowley's mobile technology dreams was found in the new generation of smartphones. In 2007, Apple CEO Steve Jobs made history when he unveiled his company's revolutionary new device. It was unlike any mobile phone the world had seen before. According to Jobs, it wasn't a phone at all. "Today, Apple is going to reinvent the phone," Jobs said. "An iPod, a phone and an Internet communicator . . . these are not separate devices. This is one device, and we are calling it iPhone."[37]

> **"An iPod, a phone and an Internet communicator . . . these are not separate devices. This is one device, and we are calling it iPhone."** [37]
>
> —Steve Jobs, Apple co-founder

With the iPhone, a new era of mobile computing had arrived. Not only was the iPhone more powerful and capable than previous handheld devices, but it was always connected to the internet using cellular service or Wi-Fi technology. This meant people could browse websites, send text messages, and share photos as quickly and easily on a phone as they could on a laptop or personal computer. iPhones were also GPS-enabled, which meant that they could use the satellite-based Global Positioning System (GPS) to detect the phone's location anywhere in the world. Apple's iPhone caused a shift in the mobile phone industry. Other companies, including Samsung and Google, rushed to create similar devices to match the new demand.

APPS CHANGE THE GAME

In 2008, Apple added a feature that would eventually reshape the software and video game industries forever—the App Store, an online marketplace where users could download additional apps for the iPhone. Developers flocked to create new software and games to sell to excited customers, and soon the App Store expanded from 500 apps to more than 1 million. Google quickly followed with its own market, Google Play, to bring many of the same apps to customers using phones running the competing Android operating system.

By creating an app or game for Apple's iOS or Google's Android, developers could take advantage of the advanced features offered in these powerful, pocket-sized devices. They could also market their apps to smartphone users across the globe. They imagined endless new ways for people to interact with information—and each other—as they moved around the world. Social networks such as Facebook and Twitter took advantage of mobile technology, and new social apps like Instagram were designed with mobility in mind. Smartphone technology transformed internet use and communications.

For Crowley, it was time to put his idea for a location-based game into action. In 2008, he teamed up with another developer, Naveen Selvadurai, to invent a new app called Foursquare, which launched in 2009. Instead of relying on text messages about someone's whereabouts, like Crowley's Dodgeball game, Foursquare could use GPS to detect exactly where someone was located and offer helpful information about nearby points of interest. The app also allowed friends to communicate with each other.

With Foursquare, Crowley created a game-like service that rewarded people for visiting their favorite real-world locations more often than their friends or for sharing helpful tips and recommendations about the places they go. The most active users would earn badges for their achievements, such as the "Gym Rat" badge that was unlocked after several check-ins to a fitness center. The most successful players of Foursquare would even be crowned the "mayor" of their favorite hangout spots. This blending of game features into real-world activities is known as gamification. Soon, data that Foursquare's players were sharing about businesses, shopping, and other activities became a valuable resource for the app.

Thanks to the mobile phone industry, video games now reach more people and places than ever before. In fact, games for mobile phones and tablets make up more than 40 percent of the video game market. Many of the games played on mobile devices are referred to as casual games. This means that they are played in short bursts of time throughout the day, with an overarching storyline or challenge played over a long period of time. Instead of dedicating hours to a game until it is completed, which is common with console and PC games, casual gamers spend as little as a few minutes a day working on a single level or challenge. Casual gaming often happens during moments of free time, such as while waiting in line, during an airplane flight, or before falling asleep at night.

Zynga was one of the first companies to capitalize on the potential of casual gaming. Among its many popular titles is the hugely successful *FarmVille*. In this farming simulation, players are challenged to plant and harvest crops, raise animals, sell their goods, and maintain a successful farming enterprise. This process takes time—often much more time than playing a console game—but the game is never played all at once. It requires players to come back periodically to complete small tasks that keep their farms running smoothly. "The most addictive of Facebook games is hardly even a game—it's

Some apps "gamify" real-world activities by offering rewards or items for visiting different locations. Someone who checks in to the app at a park might receive a badge for being outside or visiting a monument.

more a series of mindless chores on a digital farm," one reviewer wrote in *Time* magazine. "How many hours of lost productivity does that translate to? Tough to guess. But for me, personally, at least dozens."[38]

GAMES AND SOCIAL NETWORKS

Many mobile games, including *FarmVille*, are tied directly to a player's social network through platforms like Facebook. Players are rewarded for sharing their progress and recommending the game to their friends. This type of social interaction helps keep players interested in improving their performance. It also brings in many new customers for game developers. *Customers* may be a better word than *players* in this case due to another feature that was pioneered by Zynga—microtransactions. Although *FarmVille* and similar games are technically free-to-play (F2P), there are many optional items available for purchase inside the game. These microtransactions, also called in-app purchases, make it possible to get ahead in a game, or level up, with less time and effort. Prices can range from ninety-nine cents to more than twenty dollars.

The social-network element of these mobile games motivates players to reach higher levels than their friends and to post their progress on social media. This leads to a lot of profits from microtransactions for game developers like Zynga. Some people have criticized these games for being too addictive by design and too focused on making money. "It's only about exploiting the players. [*FarmVille*] actually makes people worry about it when they're away . . . which previous genres of game never did," said game developer Jonathan Blow.[39]

> **"[FarmVille] actually makes people worry about it when they're away . . . which previous genres of game never did."** [39]
>
> —*Jonathan Blow, game developer*

PORTABLE PRESENCE

Mobile gaming technology has helped video games feel increasingly interactive and real. Since the arrival of the iPhone and iPad, most mobile phones and tablets have shared a common set of features, including a touch screen, few or no physical buttons, and a variety of internal sensors that detect information about the phone's environment. With these features, the act of playing a mobile game becomes a distinctly physical experience. A player might slide his finger across the screen to launch an attack on enemies in *Angry Birds* or to slice up some flying fruit in *Fruit Ninja*. Perhaps a player tilts the phone from left to right, engaging the internal accelerometer, in order to guide her character through obstacles in *Doodle Jump*. Someone might even shake their phone, tap it vigorously, speak or sing into the microphone, listen for sounds, or feel for vibrations. All of these actions involve using physical senses while playing a game.

People remain aware of their surroundings when playing a casual mobile game. However, some games use players' specific locations, along with mobile gaming technology, to create an experience that blurs the line between the game and the real world. These location-aware apps are sometimes called augmented reality (AR) games. By using data from a smartphone's GPS sensor, information from the internet, and the phone's camera, AR games create a game world all around gamers. People can see and interact with these games using their phones as a window into the virtual world.

One of the first AR games, made available for mobile users in 2012, was called *Ingress*. It was developed by a longtime Google employee named John Hanke and his team at Niantic Labs, a gaming company he started within Google. Years earlier, Hanke had helped create Google Maps, which is now one of the company's most successful products. Google Maps powers the GPS navigation features on smartphones and computer systems all over the world.

HAPTIC FEEDBACK

Some smartphones vibrate when people type or press the touch screen. Some video game controllers rumble when there's an explosion in the game. These are examples of haptic feedback, or haptics, which provide a realistic sense of touch or physical feeling to go along with a virtual experience.

Haptic feedback goes back to the 1970s, when an arcade motorcycle game developed by Sega would vibrate when players ran into other bikers. The technology arrived in the world of mainstream home gaming in 1997, when Nintendo introduced the Rumble Pak accessory for the Nintendo 64. The device plugged into the controller and vibrated in time with in-game explosions, gunshots, and other actions. Later controllers for the PlayStation and Xbox had built-in vibration functionality. The latest innovation, present in the Nintendo Switch console released in 2017, is a feature Nintendo calls HD Rumble. The feature combines motion sensors with vibration motors that can provide feedback ranging from subtle to intense. Nintendo demonstrated HD Rumble with a game that involves shaking the controller as if it were a glass with ice cubes in it. The company said players would be able to use the haptic feedback to determine how many ice cubes were present.

When Niantic launched *Ingress* for Android devices in 2012, it was a unique game that took advantage of the vast amounts of location data in Google Maps to transform the real world into a video game.

Ingress is a science fiction adventure about mysterious creatures that are opening up energy portals all over the world. Players can choose to work with one of two teams in the game. Players use their smartphones to view the locations of portals on a map. They must then travel to the corresponding real-life location—often a local landmark, such as a statue or artwork in a public park—in order to take the portal away from the other team. It takes a lot of effort, and a lot of teamwork, to be successful at playing *Ingress*. "No small amount of travel is necessary if you really want to immerse yourself," noted one reviewer, "and you'll need friends both new and old to climb [the] ranks."[40]

The AR technology of *Ingress* was impressive, but it was the social side of the game that seemed to attract the most attention. A player from China said, "*Ingress* is all about being offline, and people have to move out of their house to play. This is exactly what I like about the game. I want to explore every corner of my city."[41] That's also what Hanke liked most about his creation. "We're spicing up real life," he told technology website *VentureBeat* in 2014. At that time, *Ingress* had reached 2 million players. "For personal happiness and all that, just walking and moving and exercising," he said, "a lot of the positiveness that people associate with *Ingress* is partly due to that."[42]

While playing *Ingress* is a positive experience for many of its fans, there are some downsides to using gaming to interact with the real world. Since players often team up in real life to visit portals or spy on the opposing team, they must take the risk of revealing their identities to people they've met online. In some cases, players have encountered dangerous people or areas of their cities, especially at night. Some have even been seriously injured in accidents while playing *Ingress*, and one player in Ireland tragically drowned while attempting to reach a landmark in the game. Others have been questioned by police for appearing suspicious while interacting with *Ingress* portals.

MORE AND MORE AR

Ingress was only the beginning of AR. In 2013, Brandon Badger of Niantic Labs said, "My hope is that there would be hundreds of these types of games. We're playing a sci-fi secret agent game, but there could be fantasy games, superhero games, zombie games. We could

Niantic used some elements of Ingress *to create their next hit game,* Pokémon Go. *The game uses maps and location data to help guide players to nearby Pokémon.*

all be playing these games in the same physical space, but in different virtual worlds."[43]

Niantic's next step in the world of AR was to bring mobile gaming back to its origins, with Pokémon. In 2016, Niantic unveiled *Pokémon Go* in partnership with Nintendo. Using the location database that Niantic had developed for *Ingress* portals, millions of Pokémon were hidden all over the world, along locations called PokéStops where players could acquire in-game items. When a player discovers the location of a Pokémon, an image of the Pokémon appears on the smartphone screen as if it were standing right there in the real world. By touching the screen to throw Pokéballs, players can catch and collect the Pokémon, just like in the classic Game Boy series.

Pokémon Go was an instant phenomenon. Within hours of its release, it was the top-selling app on app stores all over the world.

Tens of millions of players signed up to play, and in less than a year these players had spent more than $1 billion on microtransactions inside the game. No game had ever sold so much so quickly. As Brian Barrett wrote for *Wired*, "In the summer of 2016, you couldn't walk two blocks without running into, sometimes literally, a person in hot Pidgey pursuit," referring to the name of one of the in-game monsters.[44] Thanks to Pokémon, suddenly the whole world knew about AR. In 2017, Apple began showcasing AR in its App Store, and the company has added special features and tools to its iPhone and iPad devices so that developers can create new AR experiences. Several popular games have taken advantage of this technology, including *Jurassic World Alive* and *The Walking Dead: Our World*, which use the smartphone camera to place terrifying dinosaurs and zombies into the streets or even the player's living room. The same technology is now being used for educational apps that can project planets, animals, and human anatomy into real spaces so that they can be examined up close.

> **"In the summer of 2016, you couldn't walk two blocks without running into, sometimes literally, a person in hot Pidgey pursuit."** [44]
>
> —*Brian Barrett, journalist*

WHAT IS THE FUTURE OF GAMING TECHNOLOGY?

Palmer Luckey had always enjoyed taking things apart. When he was young, he would open up his video game consoles to see how they worked. Eventually, Palmer's interest turned toward building large, multi-screen gaming setups. He wanted to immerse himself in the stories of games. He realized he wanted to be inside the game, not simply a player watching from the outside world. Palmer had heard about VR technology, which used video and computer technology to give users a feeling of being inside a virtual world while wearing a headset. But the only VR headsets Luckey could find were either toys or expensive military hardware used for training soldiers. Palmer decided to start buying old VR equipment he could find at government auctions and online, but the results were disappointing. "You'd read that these VR systems originally cost hundreds of thousands of dollars, and you thought, clearly if they're that expensive, they must be good," Luckey said.[45] But most of these old headsets were so slow that they made Luckey dizzy and sick when he turned his head while using them.

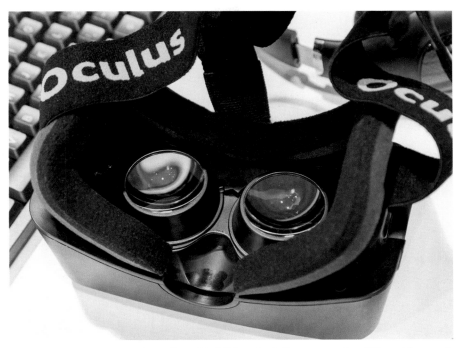

The Oculus Rift was the first affordable VR headset. Users can play different types of games from shooters to horror games to puzzle games.

From 2009 to 2012, Luckey went back to his old childhood habits and started taking apart every VR headset he could get his hands on. He discovered that the technology inside was outdated and badly designed. The display screens on smartphones were better than the ones used in these VR machines. Luckey realized he might actually be able to use a phone screen instead, but he would need to find a way to magnify the smaller screen in front of his eyes, and then use computer software to adjust the image so that it looked right.

Luckey's idea worked, and it only cost him about $300 to make. He was so excited that he posted about his results on an internet forum. To his surprise, he was soon contacted by John Carmack, the video game developer who had created the Doom series.

Carmack wanted to try the new headset, and Luckey sent him one right away. Luckey didn't know that Carmack was planning to show his work to a bunch of people at the annual E3 gaming convention, the largest trade show for the video game industry. "I was in Boston at a display conference at the time," Luckey recalled. "People there were like, 'Dude, Palmer, everyone's writing articles about your thing!'"[46] Luckey's headset, which he called the Oculus Rift, had impressed even the experts. What happened next would change Luckey's life— and the gaming world—forever.

THE QUEST FOR A NEW EXPERIENCE

Luckey wasn't the only one searching for a better gaming experience. Game developers and players had been dreaming for decades about the promise of VR. However, so many attempts had failed that a lot of people assumed VR devices were never going to be effective for gaming. Instead of chasing after virtual experiences they couldn't make, some electronics companies developed different types of immersive technologies instead. One of Nintendo's former company presidents, Hiroshi Yamauchi, said, "Doing the same things as others will get you nowhere in the entertainment business."[47] These words became the guiding philosophy during development of Nintendo Wii, the revolutionary game console released in 2006.

Unlike the competing game systems of its time, the Wii was not focused on high-end graphics or complicated games. Instead, Nintendo decided to immerse players with interactive experiences that required physical motion. To accomplish this, the traditional game controller was abandoned in favor of a rod-shaped remote control that could be held in one hand. The Wii Remote was equipped with internal motion sensors. Wii games were controlled by pointing and making gestures with the remote. This allowed for a wide range of games that simulated real-world activities such as bowling and golfing.

Nintendo surprised its customers by reimagining video games as a physical and social experience. By the end of 2008, the Wii had sold more than 13 million units in the United States, which was 2 million more than the Xbox 360 and more than twice the number of PlayStation 3 sales. This success had a major impact on Nintendo, which has continued to pursue this kind of innovative game experience with its follow-up Wii U and Switch consoles.

Although the Microsoft Xbox 360 had a more powerful processor and sharper graphics, it was clear from Nintendo's success that hardcore games with advanced visuals were not the only way to excite players. Microsoft needed a way to immerse its customers in new types of games if the Xbox was to compete on this new playing field. The solution was found in a top-secret experiment known as Project Natal. "Our starting point, as gamers, was that computer games were getting boring," said Tamir Berliner, who worked on Natal. "We wanted more immersion. . . . We wanted to take it to full-body games."[48]

The goal of Project Natal was to eliminate the game controller entirely. Instead, the player would become the controller by using

> **"Our starting point, as gamers, was that computer games were getting boring. We wanted more immersion. . . . We wanted to take it to full-body games."[48]**
>
> —Tamir Berliner, Project Natal

The Kinect captures movements of the players and puts them into the video game. Because of this, movement games that involve dancing are popular for the Kinect.

body motion to interact with the game. This required not only a sophisticated 3D camera, but also software to learn and predict how a human being would move. Using cutting-edge imaging technology and AI, Alex Kipman and his team spent more than three years transforming Project Natal into a groundbreaking device called Kinect.

Released in late 2010, Kinect was sold as a peripheral, or add-on device, for the Xbox 360 game console. "We wanted to compete head-on with *Wii Sports*," said George Andreas, whose company, Rare, developed the game *Kinect Sports*. He added, "We knew we could do so much more with Kinect than you could with Wii."[49] The Kinect sensor was capable of detecting players' complex motions far beyond the capabilities of the Wii Remote. As Microsoft's Marc Whitten put it, "[It] wasn't a game controller. It was much, much broader than that."[50]

Shortly after its launch, others began to imagine the possibilities for Kinect. Universities and tech companies all over the world bought Kinect sensors for use in research projects and experiments. Professors at MIT created a gesture-based interface for controlling a computer, while researchers at the University of California-Berkeley used Kinect to pilot an autonomous drone. A company in Russia turned Kinect into an AR mirror that could show customers what they'd look like wearing different clothes. In Portugal, a scientist developed a shopping cart that followed a person in a wheelchair. Microsoft responded by releasing a software developer kit (SDK) for Kinect. SDKs are used to help others create projects that would work with the compatible device. Kinect sales skyrocketed. With more than 10 million units sold in less than one year, Kinect broke the world record to become the fastest-selling technology product in history.

These advancements reflect the growing desire to break free of the traditional screen-based experiences that have defined gaming since its earliest days. By creating new spaces for interacting with video games, new forms of entertainment may be created that appeal to an even larger audience. "We have the capability to turn your living room into a petting zoo, into a sports stadium—so our customer base is all those who have

> **"We have the capability to turn your living room into a petting zoo, into a sports stadium—so our customer base is all those who have rejected gaming either because of the content or the controller."** [51]
>
> —Matt Barlow, Microsoft

rejected gaming either because of the content or the controller," says Microsoft's Matt Barlow.[51]

VR ARRIVES

Palmer Luckey's Oculus Rift VR headset earned a lot of attention and praise. It also earned a lot of money. Less than two years after the public got its first look at Luckey's creation, his company had raised more than $2 million through the crowdfunding website Kickstarter.

A more high-profile investor was also interested in the Rift. After Facebook CEO Mark Zuckerberg got to try out the Oculus Rift in 2014, he said "[it's] one of the coolest things I've ever seen."[52] Almost immediately, Zuckerberg made Luckey an offer to buy his company for $2 billion. Oculus is now a part of Facebook and, according to Zuckerberg, an important part of the social network company's future. "Imagine enjoying a court side seat at a game, studying in a classroom of students and teachers all over the world or consulting with a doctor face-to-face—just by putting on goggles in your home," Zuckerberg wrote on his Facebook page.[53]

In Oculus, Zuckerberg sees far more than a gaming device. Facebook plans to incorporate virtual reality into future products, such as a VR social network application called Facebook Spaces. Devices like the Rift, which are known as head-mounted displays (HMD), represent the next step in the journey toward truly immersive virtual experiences. VR headsets allow users to leave their controllers, smartphones, and power cords behind.

Following the Oculus Rift, several other companies have released similar VR headsets such as the Samsung Gear. Most of these units use a smartphone as their display screens. By slipping a phone into a set of goggles, the goggles become a portable HMD. This is

The Samsung Gear VR headset uses a smartphone to display images. People can test the headset at various stores and conventions before purchasing one.

a low-cost way for many people to try VR. More advanced units must still be connected to a computer so that they can use the computer's powerful graphics card. Actions within VR games are usually performed with handheld controllers. This means that the most immersive VR experiences available today are not portable.

AR AND POINT CLOUD MAPPING

Another challenge for VR is the lack of mobility while wearing these headsets. It is difficult for users to walk around with screens strapped to their faces. For that purpose, AR may be the future of HMDs. This is the same technology that allowed for games such as *Pokémon Go*.

Although it is not a fully immersive experience, *Pokémon Go* shows how AR can display virtual elements alongside the real world. Similarly, anyone who has enjoyed using one of the face-mapping features in Snapchat or Instagram has seen the potential for this kind of technology. With the flick of a finger, suddenly a selfie can be transformed with puppy ears, bulging eyeballs, or a halo.

These AR experiences work through a technology called point cloud mapping. When the camera is pointed at an object or person, the device projects tiny dots onto its surface, sometimes using infrared lights or lasers. These infrared lights help measure the position and depth of the object and track its movement. In the case of Snapchat or Instagram filters, the app then displays features, such as the animated puppy ears, in the right spot on a photo. In the same way, a point cloud is used to map out a living room so that a Pikachu can appear on a sofa in *Pokémon Go*.

MIXED REALITY

AR and point cloud mapping will soon help create the next generation of HMDs. These devices will use transparent lenses like the ones commonly found in prescription eyeglasses. Just like mobile phones have allowed people to remain present in their surroundings while playing games on the go, mixed reality (MR) headsets will make it possible to interact with both virtual and real-life surroundings at the same time. With MR, the world around gamers becomes their display screen and, like with the Kinect, gamers themselves are the controllers. Unlike with game consoles, smartphones, or even VR headsets, mixed reality makes it possible for players to walk around inside a virtual world while staying aware of their real-world surroundings.

Mixed reality might sound like a scene from a movie, but this technology already exists. At Microsoft, Kipman moved on from the Kinect to a new mission, with the goal of taking 3D sensing technology to the next level. Released in 2016, Microsoft's HoloLens is the first mixed reality headset available to the public.

HoloLens is a new type of HMD that combines many technologies. The headset does not use a video screen like VR devices. The wearer is able to see the surrounding environment clearly through transparent lenses. HoloLens can see its surroundings too, thanks to advanced Kinect-like sensors that can create a point cloud of an entire room. At the same time, HoloLens looks inward to track the user's eyes. It can tell where the person is looking and what can be seen from that viewpoint. With that information, HoloLens then projects holographic images onto tinted lenses in front of the user's eyes, which allows the user to see a virtual layer in the real world.

It is almost impossible to tell what is real and what isn't while wearing a HoloLens. Because the device can see what the wearer sees, virtual items look as if they're hidden behind other objects or sitting on surfaces just as they would in real life. "It can see like no machine before it," wrote columnist Kevin Dupzyk, who got a chance to try out HoloLens in 2016. He added, "Those holograms—aside from their odd, shimmery essence—are truly in the scene. No longer holograms, they are real."[54]

HoloLens was available to both developers and the general public

"Those holograms— aside from their odd, shimmery essence—are truly in the scene. No longer holograms, they are real." [54]

—Kevin Dupzyk, columnist

by the end of 2016, but the technology is still very expensive. As of 2018, Microsoft was selling HoloLens headsets for up to $5,000 each. As with all new technologies, this price is sure to come down over the next several years. The HoloLens device will probably get smaller as well. As of 2018, HoloLens is similar in size to a VR headset.

Other companies are working on portable MR devices. Among the most promising of these is Magic Leap, which raised more than a billion dollars from investors for its ultra-secretive project, a mixed reality headset called Magic Leap One. A big chunk of that money, more than $500 million, has come from a single investor—Google. This massive financial contribution from one of the world's leading tech companies shows just how important MR will likely become in the near future. It might also indicate the high expectations for Magic Leap's technology. The CEO of Magic Leap, Rony Abovitz, believes that Magic Leap is for everyone. He stated that "We think it's at the border of being practical for everybody. Our whole thing with Magic Leap One is, we want people to realize this is what computing should look like — not [laptops], not TVs, not phones."[55] Magic Leap One uses technology similar to that of the Microsoft HoloLens. Slightly different images, each making up different layers of the virtual scene, are projected before the user's eyes. But the Magic Leap moves some of the hardware off of the headset and into an attached device about the size of an iPhone. This could be carried with the user, as phones are now, making the lenses lighter and easier to wear.

Once mixed reality becomes widely available to the public, it seems that there could be endless possible uses for the technology. Many common activities could become like the virtual world of games. "Rather than pulling your mobile phone in and out of your pocket, we want to create an all-day flow; whether you're going to the doctor or a meeting or hanging out, you will all of a sudden be amplified by the collective knowledge that is on the web," explains Abavitz.[56] At school, students will be able to see the people, places, and things their teacher describes right before their eyes. Virtual field trips will become a common experience

> **"Rather than pulling your mobile phone in and out of your pocket, we want to create an all-day flow; whether you're going to the doctor or a meeting or hanging out, you will all of a sudden be amplified by the collective knowledge that is on the web." [56]**
>
> —*Rony Abavitz, CEO of Magic Leap*

as well. This may look similar to a HoloLens project created at NASA's Jet Propulsion Laboratory in Southern California. There, a group of scientists and developers used detailed images of Mars taken by its *Curiosity* rover to create a fully immersive Martian environment. For the first time, researchers could walk around the surface of Mars, examine the rocks and craters, and see the red soil under their feet without ever leaving Earth.

THE MINECRAFT GENERATION

Mixed reality is expected to transform how people live, work, and play. For some, this will be a dramatic change, just as the arrival of smartphones seemed jarring to generations of people who grew up before handheld devices and internet connectivity were available. Others might gradually give up their trusty mobile devices for a new set of MR glasses, just as they once found themselves spending increasingly more time looking down at their phones. For the youngest

People in the Minecraft Generation may have an easier time working in groups because of multiplayer games. In order to win multiplayer games, people have to work together.

generation that has grown up with modern video games, using mixed reality will likely be an easy choice. They are most familiar with the virtual world and most comfortable spending time in it. Having grown up building with digital blocks in video games such as *Minecraft*, many activities of the virtual world seem very natural to today's young people. For them, hanging out in a virtual place may even feel more comfortable than the real world. That is why some people have started to call this the Minecraft Generation. The name describes young people who have learned to communicate, socialize, and create inside a virtual space. They are the ones who will adapt most quickly to a mixed reality future.

The Minecraft Generation already provides some indications as to what that future might look like. Perhaps the most popular format of *Minecraft* is the online multiplayer mode. For the young people who spend many hours building and exploring in that virtual world, it is very common to cooperate with other people. According to Jim Fowler, the CIO at Nationwide, his son has learned how to collaborate with others thanks to *Minecraft*. He states,

> What fascinates me about how my son and his friends build complex things together is that nobody is really in charge, yet everything gets built, quickly and completely, with changes made as needed along the way. . . . Just imagine what will be possible when my son's generation enters the workforce.[57]

The creations these Minecrafters make are shared by the thousands on YouTube, where these videos have millions of views. From this, it seems that the future for the Minecraft Generation will be one filled with collaboration, creativity, and sharing.

BLURRING REAL AND VIRTUAL WORLDS

Mixed reality has already arrived in *Minecraft*. There is a VR version that can be played with a head-mounted display such as Samsung Gear VR or the Oculus Rift. This turns the blocky environments of *Minecraft* into an immersive world. Fowler says, "players can look down over *Minecraft* landscapes superimposed on surfaces in their immediate real-world environment and see other players as tiny avatars walking around."[58] With HoloLens and mixed reality, the *Minecraft* world could merge with the real world. *Minecraft* creations could be built in spaces where people live and work. Soon it may be common for people see these virtual blocks everywhere they go—as long as they're wearing their MR glasses. One day, people may even be able to interact with the mixed reality world without the need for a mouse, touchscreen, or controller.

Hands-free interaction is the final step toward a future in which virtual objects and places become as real to people as the physical world around them. To make this possible, MR systems will need to see their users as well. That will be done with eye-tracking technology and AI. AI is programming that allows a computer to learn from past experiences, just as a human can. For example, when people interact with an AI computer, the system will keep track of the choices it makes and how the user responds. Actions that work well and achieve results the user desired will be repeated again in the future. On the other hand, mistakes are noted, corrected, and later avoided. Over time, the AI system learns about its user's wants and needs.

Eye-tracking technology is expected to be essential in a mixed reality future. While wearing an MR headset, the device will use AI

VIRTUAL REALITY, REAL VOMIT

One of the biggest problems with virtual reality technology is that it makes a lot of people feel sick. After just a few minutes, it can cause dizziness and nausea, and very often it makes people vomit. This is one of the reasons why it took so long for VR to become popular and why some people thought it never would. The problem is something called latency. This is when a VR system runs too slowly to keep up with the movements of a person's head. Human brains are very sensitive to these slight delays. That is what causes motion sickness. The Oculus Rift was one of the first VR products to seriously reduce latency, which is why so many people are able to comfortably use the headset. The problem of latency has not been completely eliminated, but Oculus and other VR companies have invested a lot of money in trying to solve it.

to learn about users through their eyes. What users choose to look at, how they react, and even how they feel about the things they see can be calculated by the software. Once the MR systems have learned enough about their users, it will be possible for users to make commands just by looking around. With this technology, moving virtual objects, playing a game, or even writing a book with a virtual keyboard could be done with simple eye movements. When people are tired, happy, or angry, their MR system will know by the way their eyes look.

This world may sound imaginary and futuristic, but all of these technologies exist today, either as a product or a project in development. Some experts believe that mixed reality will be ready for the consumer market by 2025. Other technologies may be ready soon after. According to a 2017 survey of game developers by the International Game Developers Association (IGDA), 62 percent of survey respondents said that "advancement in game design . . . [was] most important to the growth of the industry."[59] With these advances will come a whole world of possibilities.

From mainframes to arcades, computers to consoles, and then mobile to mixed reality, each step has brought the real world closer to the virtual world. Soon, it may be nearly impossible to tell them apart. While experts may not know exactly where video game technology is headed, many people agree that video games are a part of the future. Kellee Santiago, founder of thatgamecompany, says, "I don't see the desire for rich, immersive, long-form game experiences going away. There will be new types of games, and new types of players, but I think there will always be a place, and a desire, for these gorgeous worlds we can lose ourselves in."[60]

SOURCE NOTES

INTRODUCTION: CREATING VIRTUAL WORLDS

1. Quoted in Damien McFerran, "Eiji Aonuma Says Zelda: Breath of the Wild Is 'Maybe the Most Fun' He's Had Making Games," *Nintendo Life*, January 29, 2018. www.nintendolife.com.

2. Quoted in Keith Stuart, "What Do We Mean When We Call a Game Immersive?" *Guardian*, August 11, 2010. www.theguardian.com.

3. Quoted in "Video Games Help Make Lifelong Friendships," *Entertainment Software Association*, n.d. www.theesa.com.

4. Tom Wijman, "Mobile Revenues Account for More Than 50% of the Global Games Market as It Reaches $137.9 Billion in 2018," *Newzoo*, April 30, 2018. www.newzoo.com.

5. Wijman, "Mobile Revenues Account for More Than 50% of the Global Games Market."

CHAPTER 1: WHAT IS THE HISTORY OF GAMING TECHNOLOGY?

6. Quoted in Robert Purchase, "Pitts Recalls Making America's First Coin-Op," *Eurogamer*, May 18, 2010. www.eurogamer.net.

7. Quoted in Gil Press, "First Successful Video Game from Atari and In-Vehicle Computer from Microsoft," *Forbes*, November 27, 2016. www.forbes.com.

8. Clive Thompson, "Clive Thompson: The Folding Game," *Guernica*, November 13, 2012. www.guernicamag.com.

9. Quoted in Chris Stokel-Waker, "Atari Teenage Riot: The Inside Story of Pong and the Video Game Industry's Big Bang," *BuzzFeed*, November 29, 2012. www.buzzfeed.com.

10. Quoted in Simon Parkin, "The Space Invader," *New Yorker*, October 17, 2013. www.newyorker.com.

11. Quoted in Mike Dolan, "Behind the Screens," *Wired*, May 1, 2001. www.wired.com.

12. Quoted in Mike Mahardy, "Collector Has First and Only English Super Mario Bros. Review," *IGN*, January 30, 2014. www.ign.com.

13. Quoted in Mahardy, "Collector Has First and Only English Super Mario Bros. Review."

14. Quoted in Brittany Vincent, "10 Things You Should Never Say to a Nintendo Fan," *Complex*, May 20, 2013. www.complex.com.

15. Quoted in Rob Crossley, "Mortal Kombat: Violent Game That Changed Video Games Industry," *BBC News*, June 2, 2014. www.bbc.com.

16. Quoted in Eben Shapiro, "Nintendo-Philips Deal Is a Slap at Sony," *New York Times*, June 3, 1991. www.nytimes.com.

17. Quoted in David Craddock, "Changing the System: How Nintendo 64 Revolutionized 3D Game Design," *Shacknews*, June 23, 2016. www.shacknews.com.

18. Aaron Curtiss, "New Nintendo 64 Is a Technical Wonder," *Los Angeles Times*, September 30, 1996. www.latimes.com.

CHAPTER 2: HOW DOES GAMING TECHNOLOGY CREATE INTERACTIVE EXPERIENCES?

19. Quoted in IGN Staff, "Ultima's Population Reaches 100,000," *IGN*, December 16, 1998. www.ign.com.

20. Quoted in IGN Staff, "Ultima's Population."

21. Allen Rausch, "World of Warcraft," *GameSpy*, December 7, 2004. www.pc.gamespy.com.

22. Tom McNamara, "World of Warcraft Review," *IGN*, December 10, 2004. www.ign.com.

23. Quoted in John McLean-Foreman, "Interview with Minh Le," *Gamasutra*, May 30, 2001. www.gamasutra.com.

24. Quoted in Andrea Peterson, "Gabe Newell on What Makes Valve Tick," *Washington Post*, January 3, 2014. www.washingtonpost.com.

25. Philip Rosedale and Cory Ondrejka, "Glimpse Inside a Metaverse: The Virtual World of Second Life," *YouTube,* March 1, 2006. www.youtube.com.

26. Rosedale and Ondrejka, "Glimpse Inside a Metaverse."

27. Rosedale and Ondrejka, "Glimpse Inside a Metaverse."

28. Quoted in Paul Sloan, "The Virtual Rockefeller," *CNN Money*, December 1, 2005. www.money.cnn.com.

29. Quoted in Chris Stokel-Walker, "Second Life's Strange Second Life," *Verge*, September 24, 2013. www.theverge.com.

30. Quoted in Daniel Goldberg and Linus Larsson, *Minecraft: The Unlikely Tale of Markus Notch Persson and the Game That Changed Everything*. New York: Seven Stories Press, 2013, p. 95.

SOURCE NOTES CONTINUED

31. Quoted in Goldberg and Larsson, *Minecraft*, p. 94.

32. Quoted in Brian Crecente, "Notch on Leaving Mojang: 'It's Not About the Money. It's About My Sanity,'" *Polygon*, September 15, 2014. www.polygon.com.

33. Quoted in Chris Plante, "The Creator of 'Minecraft' Is Leaving the Studio He Created; Read His Goodbye Letter," *Verge*, September 15, 2014. www.theverge.com.

34. Quoted in Daniel Cooper, "Microsoft Bought 'Minecraft' after a Single Tweet by Its Creator," *Engadget*, March 3, 2015. www.engadget.com.

35. Quoted in Plante, "The Creator of 'Minecraft' Is Leaving the Studio He Created."

CHAPTER 3: HOW HAS GAMING TECHNOLOGY BECOME MOBILE?

36. Quoted in ZDNet Staff, "Satoshi Tajiri—Pokemon Founder Preaches Non-Violence," *ZDNet*, April 22, 2001. www.zdnet.com.

37. Quoted in Connie Guglielmo, "10 Years Ago Today: Remembering Steve Jobs Make IPhone History," *CNET*, January 9, 2017. www.cnet.com.

38. Dan Fletcher, "The 50 Worst Inventions," *Time*, May 27, 2010. www.time.com.

39. Quoted in Simon Parkin, "Catching Up with Jonathan Blow," *Gamasutra*, December 6, 2010. www.gamasutra.com.

40. Spanner Spencer, "Ingress Review," *Pocket Gamer*, July 17, 2014. www.pocketgamer.co.uk.

41. Quoted in Stacy Blasiola, Mio Feng, and Adrienne Massanari, "Riding in Cars with Strangers: A Cross-Cultural Comparison of Privacy and Safety in Ingress," *Social, Casual, and Mobile Games: The Changing Landscape*. Eds. Tama Leaver and Michele Wilson. New York: Bloomsbury, 2016, pp. 136–148.

42. Quoted in Dean Takahashi, "Google Niantic's Ingress Aims to Make Gamers Thinner and More Social in the Real World (Interview)," *VentureBeat*, February 9, 2014. www.venturebeat.com.

43. Quoted in Christian Nutt, "Q&A: Google Glass and the Future of Geo-Location Game Ingress," *Gamasutra*, October 31, 2013. www.gamasutra.com.

44. Brian Barrett, "The Quiet, Steady Dominance of Pokemon Go," *Wired*, July 6, 2018. www.wired.com.

CHAPTER 4: WHAT IS THE FUTURE OF GAMING TECHNOLOGY?

45. Quoted in Taylor Clark, "How Palmer Luckey Created Oculus Rift," *Smithsonian.com*, November 1, 2014. www.smithsonian.com.

46. Quoted in Clark, "How Palmer Luckey Created Oculus Rift."

47. Quoted in Mirko Ernkvist, "Console Hardware: The Development of Nintendo Wii," *The Video Game Industry: Formation, Present State, and Future*. Eds. Peter Zackariasson and Timothy L. Wilson. New York: Routledge, 2012, p. 162.

48. Quoted in David Rowan, "Kinect for Xbox 360: The Inside Story of Microsoft's Secret 'Project Natal,'" *Wired*, October 29, 2010. www.wired.co.uk.

49. Quoted in Rowan, "Kinect for Xbox 360."

50. Quoted in Rowan, "Kinect for Xbox 360."

51. Quoted in Rowan, "Kinect for Xbox 360."

52. Quoted in Josie Ensor, "Oculus Rift's Palmer Luckey: 'I Brought Virtual Reality Back from the Dead,'" *Telegraph*, January 2, 2015. www.telegraph.co.uk.

53. Quoted in Clark, "How Palmer Luckey Created Oculus Rift."

54. Kevin Dupzyk, "I Saw the Future through Microsoft's Hololens," *Popular Mechanics*, November 14, 2017. www.popularmechanics.com.

55. Quoted in Adi Robertson, "I Tried Magic Leap and Saw a Failed Glimpse of Mixed Reality's Amazing Potential," *Verge*, August 8, 2018. www.theverge.com.

56. Quoted in John Markoff, "Real-Life Illness in a Virtual World," *New York Times*, July 14, 2014. www.nytimes.com.

57. Jim Fowler, "Why Minecraft Predicts the Future of Collaborative Work," *TechCrunch*, 2016. www.techcrunch.com.

58. Fowler, "Why Minecraft Predicts the Future of Collaborative Work."

59. "2017 Developer Satisfaction Survey," *International Game Designer's Association*, January 8, 2018. www.igda.org.

60. Quoted in Patrick Stafford, "What Will the Game Industry Look Like in Five Years?" *Polygon*, November 14, 2017. www.polygon.com.

FOR FURTHER RESEARCH

BOOKS

Kathryn Hulick, *Cyber Nation: How the Digital Revolution is Changing Society*. San Diego, CA: ReferencePoint Press, 2018.

Jane McGonigal, *Reality is Broken: Why Games Make Us Better and How They Can Change the World*. New York: Penguin, 2011.

Jon Peddie, *Augmented Reality: Where We All Will Live*. New York: Springer, 2017.

Carolyn Williams-Noren, *Video Games and Culture*. San Diego, CA: ReferencePoint Press, 2019.

INTERNET SOURCES

Richard Cobbett, "The Legacy of Quake, 20 Years Later," *PC Gamer*, July 21, 2016. www.pcgamer.com.

Alex Cox, "The History of Minecraft," *TechRadar*, June 13, 2018. www.techradar.com.

Kevin Dupzyk, "I Saw the Future Through Microsoft's Hololens," *Popular Mechanics*, November 14, 2017, www.popularmechanics.com.

David M. Ewalt, "Palmer Luckey: Defying Reality," *Forbes*, January 5, 2015. www.forbes.com.

Andrea Peterson, "Gabe Newell on What Makes Valve Tick," *Washington Post*, January 3, 2014. www.washingtonpost.com.

RELATED ORGANIZATIONS AND WEBSITES

Entertainment Software Association

601 Massachusetts Ave. NW, Suite 300
Washington, D.C. 20001
www.theesa.com

The Entertainment Software Organization (ESA) is an organization that represents the US video game industry.

International Game Developers Association

150 Eglinton Ave. E, Suite 402
Toronto, ON M4P 1E8 Canada
www.igda.org

The International Game Developers Association (IGDA) is a professional organization for people who create video games.

National Aeronautics and Space Administration

300 E. Street SW, Suite 5R30
Washington, D.C. 20546
www.nasa.gov

The National Aeronautics and Space Administration (NASA) is a government agency that handles space technology and travel, including VR developments for future space missions.

World Health Organization

Avenue Appia 20
1211 Geneva 27, Switzerland
www.who.int

The World Health Organization (WHO) is the authority for international health in the United Nations. It sets standards and provides support as well as monitoring on world health crises.

INDEX

INDEX CONTINUED

IMAGE CREDITS

ABOUT THE AUTHOR

Anthony J. Rotolo was a college professor for more than ten years, teaching at Syracuse University. He taught courses in technology and media, including the very first college class on social media. He is now studying for a PhD in psychology and researching how social media affects people and society.